CW00641218

CALLIGRAPHY

Written and designed by Meme Design.

KUDOS

Published by Kudos, an imprint of Top That! Publishing plc.
Copyright © 2004 Top That! Publishing plc,
Tide Mill Way, Woodbridge, Suffolk, IP12 IAP, UK
www.kudosbooks.com
Kudos is a Trademark of Top That! Publishing plc

contents

introduction

You have probably looked at 'professional' calligraphy and thought that you could never produce anything as beautiful yourself. Like most people you may not consider yourself to be artistic enough but this book will enable your creativity to come to the fore.

The Chinese believe that mastering the art of calligraphy is an essential part of a well-rounded education, and the mark of a respected person. Calligraphy is still widely practised throughout China, and it is not necessary to be able to understand what these wonderful pieces say to appreciate their beauty.

With advice on what equipment to buy, how to use it, and even how to make money from your new skill, this book will be your entry into the ancient art of beautiful writing.

history of calligraphy

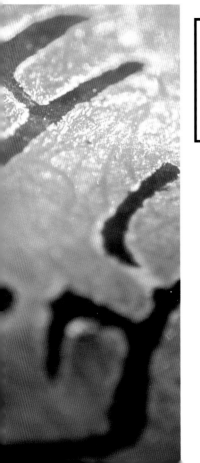

The word calligraphy comes from the Greek 'kale graphe', which means 'beautiful writing'. There are three main styles of calligraphy today: Chinese (Oriental), Arabic and Western. These styles developed independently, but, as early manuscripts spread around the world, styles began to influence each other.

the evolution of calligraphy

All calligraphy evolved from ancient forms of writing such as Egyptian hieroglyphics and Chinese pictograms. In early society the ability to read and write was the domain of the priests or other religious scholars and, as such, most writing was devoted to religious texts and subjects.

The desire to produce 'beautiful writing' came from the belief that the word of God was sacred, and that the expression of God's word should be suitably beautiful.

The ultimate expression of this belief is found in the illuminated manuscripts of the medieval monks who produced masterpieces such as the Irish *Book of Kells*.

Calligraphy, however, has never been a purely Christian practice.

Islamic scholars laboured to produce copies of the Qur'an using exquisite gold inks and rich colours. Islam's proscription on depicting images of living creatures meant that calligraphy from the Arabic lands developed a unique graphic language of pattern and colour. While Western decorative styles were based around local flora and fauna.

Today, modern Arabic script shows its calligraphic heritage clearly in its organic letter forms and elegant flourishes.

Chinese calligraphy is probably the oldest form of calligraphy, with some scholars dating it at over 4,000 years old. While languages such as English, Russian and Japanese are based around representing sounds (phonetic), Chinese and ancient Egyptian scripts represent meaning (ideographic). Chinese is the only surviving ideographic language and, as such, is uniquely suited to the expressiveness of calligraphy.

the Fall and Rise of calligraphy

The invention of the printing press removed the need for individually hand-lettered books, but for many years early printing could not match the fine detail of the best calligraphy, and skilled calligraphers remained in demand. However, as presses improved, calligraphy retreated more and more into the domain of amateurs and artists.

Another, less dramatic, technical change was the introduction of the round-nibbed pen, similar to the modern fountain pen. This change from the flat, square nibs that had been in use before made it difficult to achieve calligraphic letter forms in everyday writing. Therefore, the skill began to die out.

In China, calligraphy, along with poetry and painting, is still considered an essential indication of character. In imperial times, positions in the Court and government were allocated to those who could produce perfect writing as it was considered that someone unable to compose precise, legible writing was not to be trusted with such important matters as taxation and accounting!

Ancient Chinese masters of calligraphy are as revered today as they were generations ago. It is accepted that there are four great schools of calligraphy – Yan, Liu, Ou and Zhao – each with their own distinctive character.

ART FORM

Today calligraphy is a popular and growing hobby but it is not just limited to this. There are traditions in Japan of new students writing large calligraphic characters on huge banners at the beginning of the school year. Calligraphy is still considered an art form, not just in Asia, but all over the world.

The ability to produce beautiful writing in an age when most letters are typed, and e-mail is more widespread, is becoming recognised as a valuable skill. With the whole history of calligraphy available to the practitioner as inspiration, new forms are being created. In our modern computer era it may be that calligraphy begins to enjoy a new golden age.

an antique inkwell and pen

7

equipment

One of the delights of calligraphy is how simple it is to get started. A selection of good quality calligraphy pens, ink, paper and a flat surface to work on are all that are required.

pens

The pen is at the heart of all calligraphy. All calligraphic pens have nibs that can produce the characteristic thick and thin lines of the letter forms. Pens are available for both left- and right-handers. Right-handed pens have a straight-edged nib, while left-handed pens are angled to take into account how they will be held. It is best to try out a pen before buying, if you can. You should look for a pen that produces a good strong contrast between thick and thin lines.

A good option for beginners is to use a felt-tip pen with a calligraphic nib. Felt-tips are easier to handle and make less mess, as well as delivering a more controlled supply of ink. Of course, they also do away with constant refilling. Once they run out you simply dispose of the pen.

an old-style dipping pen

Fountain pens with calligraphic nibs appeal to the more traditionally minded. While the nibs are generally of higher quality than felt-tip pens, they do require careful maintenance. Fountain pens are available with either cartridges or reservoirs. Cartridge pens are generally cheaper and offer a range of ink colours to choose from. Both types require cleaning after use to prevent dried ink from clogging the nib.

Experienced or ambitious calligraphers will choose a dip-nibbed pen. These pens commonly consist of a wooden shaft and a selection of interchangeable nibs. These nibs have to be constantly dipped into the ink. Dipping pens are able to use thicker inks such as Chinese and Japanese ink sticks, that produce rich blacks and dense colours. These inks are not suitable for use with cartridge pens.

Chinese calligraphers favour brushes as they suit the letter forms of the Chinese alphabet. Brushes are very hard to master though and in the rest of this book we will be focussing on pen-based techniques.

ink

If you are using felt-tip pens you won't need any ink as they come pre-filled, but if you have any other sort of pen, you will need to consider what ink to use.

Always make sure that the ink you choose is suitable for the type of pen you will be writing with. Dipping pens offer the widest choice of ink types – from standard inks through to gouache paint and ink sticks.

Gouache is mixed with water to the desired consistency and can be mixed together to create a wide range of colours.

Ink sticks are also mixed with water which is traditionally done on an inkstone, which are available from most craft shops.

a Chinese ink stick and brush pen

PAPER

Paper is the third member of the calligraphic trinity. At the most basic level, any paper will do, but it is best to use a paper that does not bleed (that is, allow the ink to seep through to the other side of the paper).

For beginners, or when practising, inkjet or photocopier paper is perfectly suitable, but you will want to use a better quality paper to show off your final creations to best effect.

The finest calligraphy should be displayed on the highest-quality paper. Ancient calligraphers often wrote on parchment or vellum (made from animal hides). These may be hard to find today but most craft shops will stock ranges of fine or handmade papers that will be just right for that special project.

For a different feel you can also consider using fabrics or other materials, but these are likely to require specialist nibs.

writing on a parchment scroll

BEFORE YOU STARt

To produce the most beautiful calligraphy possible, you have to prepare yourself and your work area. Make sure all your materials are to hand, and remove any distractions such as the telephone. Take a deep breath and enjoy!

GEtting READY to WRItE

To produce the neatest writing it is necessary to be sitting comfortably. A sloping board will help you to sit up straight.

The best angle between your pen nib and the line on which you are writing is 45 degrees. This means that the ink will be drawn from your pen by the flexing of the nib and not by gravity, resulting in more controlled letter forms.

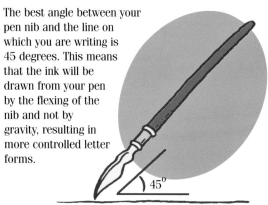

You will also need a guard sheet taped to the bottom of the board. This allows the paper you are writing on to slide underneath, so that your hand remains in the same place all the time. Ideally this should be at about shoulder height.

You should also make sure that you have a good source of even and bright light so you can see what you are writing clearly and to avoid eye strain.

Ancient calligraphers worked many long and hard hours at their manuscripts. You, however, should try to take regular breaks to avoid backache, wrist strain and other injuries.

13

How to hold the pen

Left- and right-handed people hold the pen in different ways. You may be surprised to know that the grip you use in normal writing is perfectly suitable for calligraphy.

ERGONOMICS

It is very important that you sit well when you are practising calligraphy. There is a story of a traditional calligrapher, Tang, who sat crooked and became a hunchback! Ensure that your back is straight, that you are not leaning on your arms and that your head is not too far forward.

As you gain confidence, you may find that you can control the pen best if you allow the pen body to rest against your knuckle, instead of in the 'V' between the thumb and forefinger. Your grip should be firm and still, allowing the nib to glide over the paper without pressing down on the pen.

When you write with a normal pen you can move it in any direction. A calligraphy pen will only write in certain directions – it will not move upwards or to the left if you are writing with a right-handed pen, or to the right if you are using a left-handed pen.

To form the letters correctly you need to use separate strokes. Following the numbered sequence of arrows on the samples of writing in this book will show you which strokes you need to form each letter.

your first efforts

There's one more hurdle to jump before producing your first words and letters. In order to get a feel for how your pen actually writes, the basic line strokes shown opposite will allow you to experience the sensation of making calligraphic marks on paper for the first time.

Use a few sheets for practice. Don't worry about the occasional blob or scratch – just adjust the angle of your nib or pen and keep going.

LETTER BASICS

*Now it's time to look at some actual letters.
It might all sound a bit technical but remember,
there are no hard and fast rules, only guidelines.
If it looks right to you, then that's fine.*

HEIGHT OF LETTERS

The height of your letters will depend on how wide your nib is. The wider the nib, the larger the letters. To work out how tall to make your letters, create a nib ladder by turning your paper sideways. Draw short alternate strokes on the edge of the paper as shown.

The height of the capital letters and ascenders (where part of the letter goes up e.g. b, d, t) should be slightly less than twice the size of the body of the letter. The descenders (where part of the letter goes

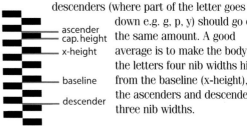

down e.g. g, p, y) should go down the same amount. A good average is to make the body of the letters four nib widths high from the baseline (x-height), and the ascenders and descenders three nib widths.

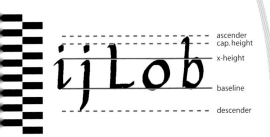

ascender
cap. height
x-height
baseline
descender

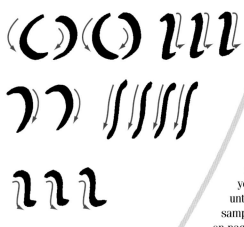

Of course you can vary this, for example making the body five nib widths and the ascenders and descenders four nib widths. The height of these lower-case letters is called the x-height, because it is based on the height of the lower-case letter x.

The chart on the left shows the relative heights of letters and their component parts. Capital letters are normally slightly lower than the ascender heights. The bowls of the letter o and other similar letters should rest slightly under the baseline to avoid a floating look.

LETTER FORMS

These practice letter forms (pictured left) show many of the basic shapes that you will need to master the style of your choice. Follow the directions as indicated by the arrows to familiarise yourself with these forms, and practise them until you can do them with ease. You can see samples of complete alphabets in various styles on pages 20–23.

First practice

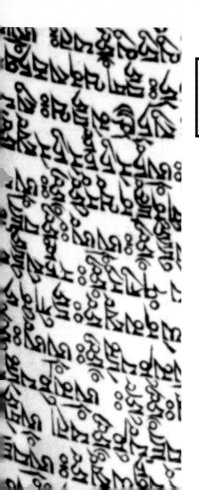

> *Now that you've got used to holding the pen, and the way it writes, it's time to start practising writing some actual letter forms.*

Practice makes perfect

The most beautiful calligraphy has perfectly uniform letters. To achieve this in your own work you will need to practise, using either graph paper or by drawing pencil lines on paper to ensure that your letters are all of the same proportions.

There are many different alphabets that can be used in calligraphy, or you can even make up your own, but it's best if you're a beginner to start with an easy alphabet.

Here are some examples of letter forms for you to practise. In each case, take your time, and remember that this is only for practice, so it doesn't matter if you smudge the ink or if you make a mistake.

The arrows show you where to start and in which direction to move your pen. Keep practising until you are happy with your efforts before going on to a complete alphabet.

m¹ ²d ³ d¹ u² ¹

v¹ ² w² ⁴ x¹ ² ³

h¹ ² p¹ ² ³

R¹ ²

19

alphabets

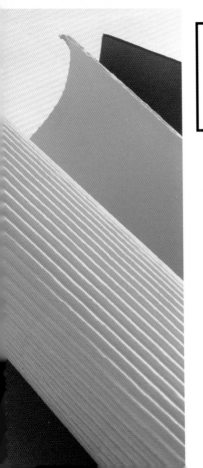

There are many possible alphabets for you to write with. However, at first, it is best to familiarise yourself with the simpler letter forms. Once you are confident producing these, you can move on to more demanding alphabets.

italic alphabet

The italic alphabet is easy to read and fairly easy to learn. The letters are quite narrow, and have oval curves. The slope of the letters can vary, so find a slope that suits you but make sure it is consistent in all the letters.

Roman capitals

These classical capital (also called majuscule) letters are based on those found on Trajan's Column in Rome, built in AD 114 to celebrate the emperor's victory over the Dacians. They work well with many forms of lower case (or minuscule) letters.

abcdefghijklm
nopqrstuvwxyz

ABCDEFGHIJKLM
NOPQRSTUVWXYZ

ABCDEFGHIJ
KLMNOPQRST
UVWXYZ

21

uncials

To write this alphabet you need to change the angle of your pen so that the nib is angled more towards the horizontal (about 27 degrees). As the letters are very rounded it is best to leave plenty of space between them or they will tend to look crammed on the page.

Uncial fonts often share many letter forms between the upper and lower cases. This can make them look slightly odd to modern eyes but with care this can be translated into an interesting effect as shown below.

UNFORESEEN

gothic

This alphabet is less legible in blocks of text than either the Roman or italic alphabets, and is medieval in appearance. It is quite difficult to master. Work at a larger scale to begin with, as this will make it easier to learn the angles of the letters. The letters should be close together with little space between them when writing words. Capitals are very difficult to master, so it may be easier to use another alphabet for these, add the smallest of lines or embellishments last.

abcdefghijklmn
opqrstuvwxyz
abcdefghijklmn
opqrstuvwxyz
abcdefghijklmn
opqrstuvwxyz
ABCDEFGHIJ
KLMNOPQRS
TUVWXYZ

23

spacing

Spacing is an integral element of the art of calligraphy. To produce truly beautiful calligraphy all of the page must be considered, including the 'white space'.

spacing between letters

Once you have become expert at forming the letters, it's time to start writing words. Calligraphers look not only at the space between letters but also at the space inside the letters. The size of the letters will determine to some extent how much space should be left between them – the bigger the letters, the more space needed between them. Letters with regular down strokes are easy to space visually.

Spacing also depends on the shape of the letter. If two letters next to each other have round edges facing each other, for example 'bd', the space between them will be closer than two letters which have straight edges next to each other, for example 'db'.

A mixture of regular down strokes and circular letters in a word is spaced differently to one with only down stroke letters.

A word with a mixture of down strokes, rounded and diagonal letters would be spaced as below.

With all combinations of letters the key is consistency of spacing.

WORD SPACING

Different alphabets have different spacing, both in the letter width, and the space between the words. For example, the Gothic alphabet has narrow letters and narrow spacing, whilst Italic has rounder letters and larger spacing. As a general rule the space between words should be the same size as the letter o in the font you are using.

mintomint

LINE SPACING

How much space you leave between each line depends on how big your letters are. The minimum amount of space you need to leave is the height of the tallest letters, or those with ascenders such as d, f, h, plus the depth of the descenders in letter forms such as g, y. A small amount of additional space is also advisable to ensure the letters don't overlap. If you are writing only in capital letters, where the letters are uniform in size, you can space the lines closer together.

page layout

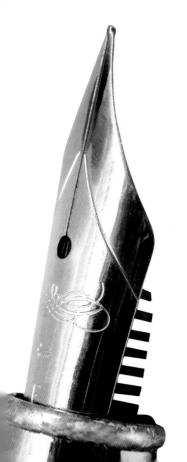

> *Now that you have the letters and spacing right, it is time to lay your words out on a page. The layout of the words on a page is just as important as the words themselves.*

preparation

Before you begin your piece, you need to think about how you are going to lay out your page. Decide on which script you are going to use, whether some of the letters or words will be larger than the others, and whether you will use colour.

The easiest way to start is with a simple layout. Choose the size of your nib depending on how much text you need to write. If there is a lot of text to fit in, choose a smaller nib size and vice versa. The general rule of layout is that the top margin will be the narrowest, and the bottom margin the widest, with the side margins somewhere between the two measurements.

If you want the lines to be more or less the same length, you can contract or expand letters or words to make them fit in.

Make sure that you leave plenty of space in the margins so that the text does not look too cramped. The easiest way of laying out the wording is with a straight margin on the left.

Regular borders, well spaced

Borders too narrow

Aligned left pages are easy to write

Centred pages make interesting shapes

Balanced pages need a visual 'spine' to work

Different letter sizes add interest

Borders too narrow, too many type sizes and too many lines all make for a bad page design

Other layouts can look more interesting, such as each line centred or balanced around a central line, giving your work a 'spine'.

Try to keep some balance to the layout, don't allow it to become too top- or bottom-heavy. Varying the size of the letters can add interest, but avoid too many changes as this does not allow for smooth reading.

Remember that simple is often the best. Overloading the page with too much text, colour, or different-sized letters and script can make the page look messy, so that it is it difficult for the reader to focus on the text.

words and pictures together make arresting layouts

illuminated letters

The early western scribes were also artists, and added colour and decoration to their work, often using the first letter of a page or paragraph to show off their skills. Look for some examples of early decorated work to see how it was done, and to develop ideas of your own.

Thinking about illumination

There are many different ways of illustrating or illuminating letters. You can either fill in the spaces within the letters, decorate them, or make the decoration actually form the letter.

To begin with you need to think about the text you are using, and relate this to the illuminated letter. For example, if the text was about spring, you could decorate the letters with flowers. Think also about the letter shape. If it is elongated, such as an f, this could be extended downwards to form a border for the paragraph. Letters containing a space, whether open or closed, can be filled with colour or a pattern.

Some letters, such as o, e or n, can be enclosed in a box or square, and the inner space decorated. The letter can either be left plain or worked into the overall design.

A decorated majuscule

An illustrated majuscule in a box

A highly decorative uncial from the *Book of Kells*

planning your decorations

At first, your decoration should be simple. It is best to design your letter in rough first, trying to keep it as near to the finished size as possible. Try to allow the decoration to flow freely, and stick to one or two patterns to begin with. As you become more skilled at illustrating letters, your decoration can become more complex.

Once you are happy with your illustration you can transfer it onto the finished page. It is usually best to do this in pencil first, so that you can correct any mistakes. Once this is done the work can be decorated using pencil, ink or paint.

Consider the overall effect of the illustration, and whether you will be adding other illustrated letters or borders to your work. Remember, it is better to under-decorate than over-decorate.

Headings

> *The heading of a piece of writing is important not only in its wording, but also because of where you place it on the page. An interesting, well-placed heading will encourage reading of the script. It needs to stand out from the rest of the text, so that it is the first thing to capture the reader's attention.*

Headings can be emphasised in different ways. Whether you choose to make the lettering bold, colourful, elaborately decorated or to combine several of these elements, it should stand out from the rest of the text. Headings should be placed slightly apart from the main wording but they don't always have to be at the top of the text. For example, you could run a heading down one side, or place it at the bottom of the page, or even run it obliquely across the middle of the piece.

Planning the page

Before writing out your piece, it is best to design the page first, deciding what the heading should be, how big to write it, and where to place it. Work it out in rough first, so that you can balance all the elements. Rule off the area that will contain the text to get a feel for the finished effect.

Straightforward headings and subheadings

Experiment with your layouts to achieve a good balance

Try using landscape layouts

subheadings

If you are including subheadings in your text, think about how they will relate both to the heading and to the rest of the text.

Try to link your ideas so that the heading and subheadings have something in common. For example, use the same decoration or style of writing for the subheading as you used for the heading, but make it smaller and simplify the decoration.

overdoing it

When adding in headings and subheadings try to remember that the purpose of these will be to increase the legibility of your work.

Too many, or ill-planned, subheadings will only serve to confuse your piece, making it harder to read. Likewise, changing font style too many times will make the piece look fragmented. If in doubt, remember the motto 'less is more'.

BORDERS

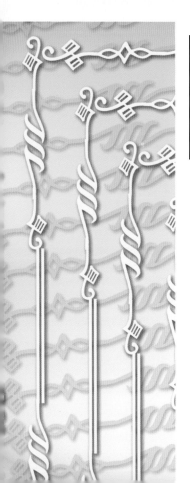

Placing a border around your calligraphy text can add greatly to the overall appearance of the piece. Before placing a border around your work you need to decide whether this will complement, and not detract from, the overall effect. If you feel that it will be of benefit, then some additional planning of the layout and design is needed.

First decide what sort of border you are going to use – is it going to surround the text completely? Will it be regular or irregular? How will the corners work? If your border is going to surround the text, either partially or completely, the best place to start is at the corner.

There are three basic ways of organising the corners of your borders; oblique, square and joggled mitre. The type to use will depend on your design and the style of border you are producing.

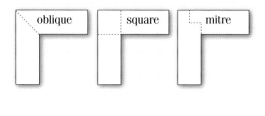

Pattern borders can be enlivened with careful use of spot colours

Use shapes to evoke the theme of your piece. For example, wave shapes around a poem about the sea

Using colour with letter borders helps to distract from the letter forms, making them into shapes

Numbers can make interesting, interlocking shapes

ROUGH IT OUT

Design your border in rough first, pencilling in the areas or spaces where the text will be, then work out your border size and design around this. Try experimenting with different tools and colours to see the different effects you can create. Use either a single tool (for example, brush or pen) or colour, or a combination of tools and/or colours, and let your creativity flow.

WHAT TYPE OF BORDER?

The type of border you use should relate in some way to the piece of writing, whether it reflects some elements of the subject matter or the style of writing used. There are many different elements of border design including spots, horizontal, vertical, oblique and lettered. These can be used singly or in combination to produce a pattern. If you choose a lettered border make sure you pick letters that work well together visually.

FLOURISHES

> *Once you've become experienced at forming the basic letter shapes, you can try your hand at flourishes. These are elaborate extensions of letters. They may be added to one or more characters in a piece of writing, and are often used for formal texts, but can feature anywhere to add flair to the piece.*

When creating flourishes bear the following points in mind:

- Your basic letter shapes must be well-formed, and the flourish should be an extension of the letter and not an addition to it.

- Flourishes should reflect the nature of the text you are writing, and should appear to be part of the natural flow of the piece.

- Make sure that the letter is legible and that the flourish doesn't obscure any other letters.

- When planning the layout of your work, take into account any flourishes that you are going to make, considering where they are going to be, and how much space they will take up.

These flourishes are similar to those often found on bank notes

Spirals make interesting flourishes

You can easily build the basic shapes into more complex ones

Remember to lift your pen when you reverse direction

Interlocking or overlapping flourishes make interesting shapes

PRACTISING FLOURISHES

You will need plenty of practice to produce flourishes with ease.

Start by practising crossing thick and thin lines, running them both diagonally and parallel to each other.

Try to keep your hand relaxed so that the lines flow naturally. Thin strokes are normally formed with an upward stroke, while thicker strokes can be made by applying more pressure on downward strokes. Begin with simple shapes before going on to more elaborate designs.

A selection of shapes to practise is shown on this page. Once you are confident with the feel of flourishes you can add them to the letter forms of your choice.

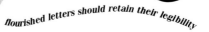

flourished letters should retain their legibility

NUMERALS

If you are going to be using numbers in calligraphy, some thought needs to be given to how they are going to fit in with the rest of the text. The numbers should blend with the letters to keep the piece balanced, and not disrupt the flow of the text.

PLACING NUMERALS

There are different ways of placing numerals effectively into a text. This will depend to some extent on the type of writing that you are using.

If the lettering is all in capitals, putting numbers of the same height into the text will camouflage them within the piece.

Some numbers can also be written partly above or below the main body of the letters, just as ascending and descending letters are. The even numbers 4, 6 and 8 can be treated like ascenders, while the numbers 3, 5, 7 and 9 can be written like descenders.

Keep the numbers the same size as the letters, so that the natural flow of the text is maintained.

Numerals as descenders

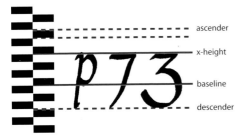

ascender
x-height
baseline
descender

Numerals as ascenders

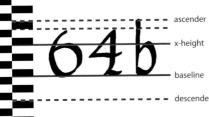

ascender
x-height
baseline
descender

Numerals at the capital height

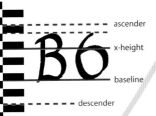

ascender
x-height
baseline
descender

Using numbers

Using numbers within your design can add interest to the layout if done well.

The letter forms of most numerals can easily be embellished with flourishes without losing legibility. Another trick with a collection of numbers, such as dates, is to vary the size of each number and its vertical placement to create pleasing interactions.

Look around for examples of interesting and original use of numerals and try to incorporate them into your work.

express yourself with creative use of numerals

CORRECTING MISTAKES

> *Mistakes are easy to make, but unfortunately are harder to fix. Some mistakes can be rectified, depending on what and where they are.*

One of the most common mistakes, of course, is spelling. Other possible pitfalls include inconsistent spacing, spilt ink, inconsistency of lettering or skipping lines.

One of the easiest ways to prevent making mistakes is to write the text in pencil first, check it, and then write it in ink. Practice, practice and more practice is the key to keeping your letters consistent.

Always start a page with the text, as it is easier to avoid making mistakes and to correct them if you do happen to make them.

Follow basic grammar rules when writing calligraphy, such as using capital letters appropriately.

If space is limited on a line, try to hyphenate so that the word is legible: it is more important to keep the length of your lines correct than to hyphenate in the 'correct' place. Always try to bear in mind that the end product has to be a balance between legibility and beauty.

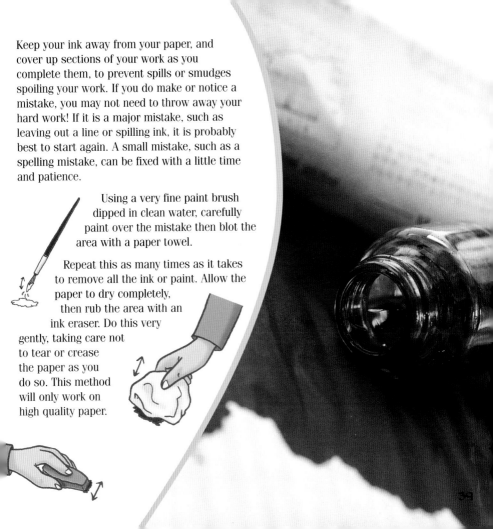

Keep your ink away from your paper, and cover up sections of your work as you complete them, to prevent spills or smudges spoiling your work. If you do make or notice a mistake, you may not need to throw away your hard work! If it is a major mistake, such as leaving out a line or spilling ink, it is probably best to start again. A small mistake, such as a spelling mistake, can be fixed with a little time and patience.

Using a very fine paint brush dipped in clean water, carefully paint over the mistake then blot the area with a paper towel.

Repeat this as many times as it takes to remove all the ink or paint. Allow the paper to dry completely, then rub the area with an ink eraser. Do this very gently, taking care not to tear or crease the paper as you do so. This method will only work on high quality paper.

CALLIGRAPHY FOR WEDDINGS

> *Why not put your newly-gained skills to good use for a wedding or other occasion? Calligraphy is ideal for invitations, name cards, menus, guest lists and much more.*

Deciding on the style and design of invitations is often the most difficult part of the project. You need to understand what sort of occasion it is going to be – will it be formal or informal? Are most of the guests family and friends, or are they business associates?

Consulting others involved in planning the big occasion will help you decide on colour schemes and the general 'feel' of your work.

Decide on the colour scheme (for example, it could match the bridesmaids' dresses), and the wording and the writing style, which can be adapted to match the formality of the occasion by adding or omitting flourishes. Be sure to carry these themes across any other items that you are producing.

If you are going to add decoration, what form will it take? Flowers and leaves, or bells and hearts, are commonly used for weddings, but by making your own invitations you can choose anything you like.

place cards

1. Make your blank place cards by cutting them out of larger sheets of card. The card should be thick enough to stand easily when folded. A good size is a 10 cm by 8 cm rectangle.

2. Score and firmly fold the card in half to make a tent shape.

3. Draw faint guide lines for the base of the letters as well as for their height (if you feel you need to).

4. Use your guest list to choose the longest name. Do this name first to give you an idea of how large to make the lettering.

5. Once you have written all the guests' names in ink, carefully rub out the pencil guide lines.

6. Remember to have plenty of spares for each item, as it is easy to make mistakes, and it may not be possible to get more of the same paper or card later.

wedding invitations

Invitations are a superb chance to show off your calligraphic skill. Don't feel you have to stick to a traditional card – you can make them in any format you (and the happy couple!) choose. You may want to make a scroll, or even a small package. In any event, you will need to start with the correct details, so be sure to check these with the bride and groom. Here is a quick guide to making an invitation that folds out.

1. Cut your invitations to shape using the guide supplied here. The finished invitation will fold into a landscape shape that will fit inside a standard envelope.

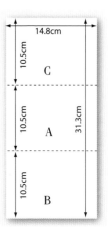

2. The centre portion (A) will be the wedding details, so sketch these out in pencil first to make sure you can fit all the words in comfortably.

3. The bottom portion (B) will be the returnable RSVP section. Again mark out all the text in pencil first. You will need to write the address that the invitation needs to be returned to on the reverse of this portion.

4. The address of the invitee will go on the reverse of portion (C).

Use the samples below as a guide for
sections A, B and C

A

B

C

hints and tips

• The invitation should reflect the
style of the occasion. There are
many styles of wedding, ranging
from very formal to very informal.
You will need to talk to those
organising the wedding to learn
what style they are aiming for.

• Formal invitations tend to have
each line centred, whereas
informal invitations may be
aligned to one side.

• If you can't find the exact
colour paper you want for the
invitations, you could consider
using coloured ink or matching
envelope lining.

• Remember to include all the
information needed – who is invited,
where the ceremony or reception will
be held, plus when it will take place. You
may need to include directions or a map.

• To make perfect folds in paper or card,
place a ruler on the fold line and then
gently score down the back of the card with a
craft knife.

• Don't forget to make thank you cards as well.

making a gift

You could put your calligraphic skills to good use and impress your family and friends by giving them handmade gifts. Why not present somebody special with a piece of poetry or prose, beautifully written and illustrated? You could present it as a scroll held with ribbon or, alternatively, frame it to hang on a wall.

First things first

The first step is to decide on the text. You may have a favourite poem or quotation in mind, or choose something from a book or magazine that inspires you. Think of the person you are going to give it to, and try to select something that is appropriate to them that you know they will enjoy.

When you have decided what you are going to write, you need to think about the colours you are going to use. The text may give you some guidance on this – for example, if it is about nature you could include greens and browns; peaceful texts lend themselves to pale blues and greens; whereas more up-beat words work well with bright yellows, reds or purples. Is the background or text going to be coloured, or perhaps both?

what style to choose

Choose the style of lettering you are going to use to match the wording. For example, uncial lettering lends itself to grand wording, while italic can be used for more modern pieces. You can mix the styles of lettering, but try not to get too complicated as the result may be difficult to read.

The size of the finished product, and the size of the lettering, are obviously linked. A good tip is to leave plenty of margin space around the text so that it doesn't look cramped. If it is going to hang on the wall, the writing needs to be large enough to read from a short distance away. If you want to use a small frame it's best to reduce the number of words on the page.

Decorating your piece

You may want to design a border or add a small illustration. This all needs to be planned before you start writing. First write out the piece in the style and sizing that you are going to use. Photocopy this and then cut out each line, laying them out on a piece of paper which is the same size as the finished

piece will be. If the lines are going to be centred, draw a line down the centre of the page and fold each line of writing in half, so that it can be placed centrally.

Draw in the margins and arrange the wording until you are happy. Roughly draw in borders or illustrations, so that you can see how they will fit in. With everything in place, draw pencil guide lines onto your chosen paper.

Now you are ready to write. Choose a time when you are feeling relaxed and will not be disturbed. Refer to your rough guide continually to avoid silly mistakes. Allow the ink to dry completely, then, very gently and carefully, rub out any pencil marks.

Finish off your masterpiece with a matching ribbon or a suitable frame, and wait for the compliments to come rolling in!

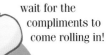

practical calligraphy

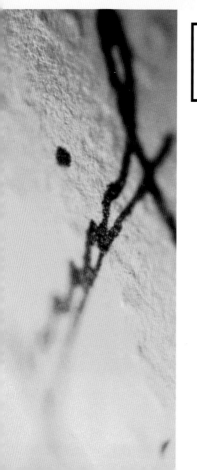

Just like the medieval monks and scribes, you now have a skill that people will want to use. But how should you go making people aware of your services?

getting the word out

You will probably find that word of mouth will work wonders. Before long your family, friends and friends of friends may well start coming to you, having heard about your talent.

More ambitious scribes may want to advertise their services. There are plenty of places to catch people's attention: in the local paper, or on small cards in local shop or post-office windows. The great thing about this is that you can use your calligraphic skills to create the advert, thus showing people how good you are!

When creating an advertisement you must bear in mind that it must be easily read. Try to give a good idea of all the ways in which people reading the advert may be able to use your services. You won't have to mention costs in your advert – that will be between you and your new clients. Don't forget to give your contact details – that sounds obvious, but it can happen!

Calligrapher

for hire

Wedding invitations
Special gifts
Thank yous
Valentine's gifts

Contact Selina Kyle
00555 4526914

See my work online:
www.penofselina.c

Decide on a size appropriate to where your advertisement will be seen – you will also need to decide on a format that will best bring out your skills, whether it's landscape, portrait or square!

Depending on where your advertisement will be placed, you may be restricted to black and white, or you may be able to use the full range of colours.

Experiment with layouts until you are happy, before committing your pen to paper.

Once finished you should send your advertisement (carefully packed!) to its final destination. You could also consider framing or laminating the advert if it is to remain in its position for sometime.

Finally, what about mixing the old and new, and putting your samples up on a website for the world to see? If you do this, you should put your web address on your advert so that people can see examples of your work before contacting you.

conclusion

Calligraphy is an ancient art in a modern world – a reminder of the craftsmanship and dedication of the scholars of days gone by and the perfect outlet for your creativity.

There are many uses for calligraphy, from invitations to presents, to advertisements, not to mention just for the pure pleasure and satisfaction of creating something beautiful. As your ability develops and your layout skills improve, you will gain the confidence to produce more ambitious projects. One of the great joys of calligraphy as a hobby is that the only limit to the work you produce is your own imagination.

In our modern world, as people turn more and more to computers and e-mail to communicate, the attraction of being able to produce beautiful hand-crafted letters can only increase.

You will also find that the concentration required in order to produce the best work acts as a great stress reliever, forcing you to take time out for yourself and your own interests.